THE OFFICIAL

ARSENAL

YEARBOOK 1994

ARSENAL

YEARBOOK 1994

Kevin Connolly

Foreword by Tony Adams

HAMLYN

CONTENTS

First published in 1994
by Hamlyn
an imprint
of Reed Consumer
Books Limited
Michelin House,
81 Fulham Road,
London SW3 6RB
and Auckland,
Melbourne, Singapore
and Toronto

ISBN 0 600 58400 3

A catalogue record for
this book is available
from the British Library

Printed and bound
in Spain

Editor: David Heslam
Designer: Richard Scott
Picture Researcher:
Jenny Faithfull
Production Controller:
Michelle Thomas

Picture
acknowledgments:

All pictures in this
book and on the cover
are reproduced by kind
permission of
Colorsport with the
exception of the pic-
tures on the following
pages which are from:

Arsenal Museum 34/35,
63 top; John Babb 37;
Mark Leech front cover
centre left; Bill Smith
16, 17, 18, 19 top, 19
bottom, 36, 36/37, 38,
39 inset, 45 bottom,
62; Max Spillmann 33
top; Topham Picture
Source/Press
Association 50.

What a great end to the season in the Cup Winners' Cup final! That night against Parma will rank alongside Mickey Thomas's winner at Anfield in my memories.

I always felt good about the final. We usually do well when we're being written off! To beat one of the top teams in Italy was an added bonus.

We had to switch our team around in Copenhagen, because of injuries and suspension. But - unlike Manchester United and Aston Villa - we didn't have to chop and change for European games because of the 'foreigners' rule. That definitely helped us in the earlier rounds.

Winning a European trophy meant a lot to all of us, especially everyone who played against Benfica. We've learned a lot since then, especially about patience and discipline in European matches.

Beating Parma was a landmark in Arsenal's history. Having tasted European success, we want more. We have two big games ahead against Milan in the Super Cup. We want to win the Cup Winners' Cup again - then go for the biggest prize of all, the Champions' Cup. That means winning the Premiership first.

That will be our top priority this season. For all our cup success, we haven't done ourselves justice in the league since 1991. We want to put that right.

I've lifted the championship trophy twice. I'd love to get my hands on it a third time!

Our youngsters completed a brilliant end to the season by winning the F.A. Youth Cup. I was an impressed spectator when they beat Millwall 3-0 to win the final 5-3 on aggregate. That was some achievement. Coming up through the youth team myself, I'm always glad to see our youngsters do well. The Youth Cup was one trophy I never got my hands on! I played in our 1983/4 team, which also included Mickey Thomas, David Rocastle, Martin Keown, Niall Quinn, Martin Hayes and Gus Caesar. But we lost to Stoke in the semi-finals.

Thanks to our fans for your great support. You were magnificent in the big European games. I'll never forget that night against Paris St-Germain.

You were a credit to the club in Copenhagen; 12,000 travelling fans, massive noise, and no bother. I hope you'll get behind us like that at Highbury in 1994/5.

Meanwhile, enjoy this book!

AUGUST

GUNNERS TAKE AIM FOR 11TH TITLE

There was a different feel to Highbury as the 1993/4 Premier League season kicked off.

The pristine new North Bank stand (minus a few seats) gleamed in the August sun. The fans filed in with high hopes. The double cup winners had taken Manchester United all the way, 1-1 in the Charity Shield the previous week, whatever the ridiculous penalty shoot-out said.

Then Coventry's 'Mr Blobby', Mick Quinn, ruined the afternoon. His 34th minute penalty put the Sky Blues ahead. Two stunning second half goals amazed David Seaman and sent the Gunners home wondering what had hit them.

ABOVE:
Tony Adams, Eddie McGoldrick, George Graham, David Seaman and Ian Wright show off the two cups in front of the new North Bank stand

Changes inevitably followed for Monday's derby at Tottenham. Martin Keown came in for the injured Lee Dixon. Ray Parlour and Eddie McGoldrick replaced Paul Merson and Anders Limpar. Sky's cameras saw Arsenal go man-for-man on Tottenham's 'diamond' formation. It was just a case of when the Gunners scored. But time was beginning to run out rapidly when Ian Wright did the business.

HAVEN'T WE MET . . .

So to Sheffield Wednesday, the team Arsenal beat in May to lift the Coca Cola and FA Cups. George Graham was purring as the Gunners dominated from the start. Kevin Campbell crossed for Wright to tap home the winner after nine minutes. Arsenal could have won by three or four.

Suddenly Graham's men were buzzing. Or were they?

The Gunners grabbed a rapid lead against David O'Leary-less Leeds thanks to Jon Newsome's first minute own goal. But the Leeds midfield took control and the Highbury fans were mightily relieved when Paul Merson netted a second 12 minutes after the break. Good job he did. Gordon Strachan pulled one back and Arsenal spent the last 20 minutes clinging on to their lead.

FOUR ON THE TROT

Everton the following Saturday came to defend. Neville Southall pulled off his usual miracles. It needed the arrival of sub Merson to lift team and crowd as the second half started. Merson cracked a post, before Wright broke the deadlock after 48 minutes. The best was yet to come. Wright raced on to Seaman's long kick, lobbed Matt Jackson, then crashed the ball past Southall for one of the goals of the season.

Four consecutive victories had wiped out the memory of those Sky Blues. Arsenal stood third in the table, poised to challenge the Red Devils from Manchester.

F.A. CARLING PREMIERSHIP

RESULTS

AUGUST 14

ARSENAL 0	COVENTRY CITY 3 Quinn (3)

AUGUST 16

TOTTENHAM H. 0	ARSENAL 1 Wright

AUGUST 21

SHEFFIELD WED. 0	ARSENAL 1 Wright

AUGUST 24

ARSENAL 2 Newsome (og) Merson	LEEDS UNITED 1 Strachan

AUGUST 28

ARSENAL 2 Wright (2)	EVERTON 0

LEAGUE POSITION

Pld	W	D	L	F	A	Pts	Pos
5	4	0	1	6	4	12	3rd

***TOP LEFT:* Ian Wright beats Peter Schmeichel to net Arsenal's Charity Shield equaliser**

***BELOW:* Ian Wright taps home the winner at Hillsborough**

SEPTEMBER

RISING UP THE TABLE

Striker Kevin Campbell burst into life and surged into the September scoring charts as the Gunners took the long road north.

If it's Wednesday, it must be Blackburn. Kevin Campbell's 75th minute goal clinched a draw in Lancashire, after Kevin Gallacher had shot Rovers into a first half lead. It was a very welcome point, after the two defeats chairman Jack Walker's multi-million pound team had inflicted on the Gunners during last year's campaign.

Ipswich put up stout resistance for 25 minutes, while Arsenal sorted out their system. Then George Graham made an inspired change, switching Paul Merson from midfield to the left flank, to try to stretch Ipswich's massed defence. Ian Wright made the breakthrough, after half-an-hour. Then Campbell enjoyed himself.

KEVIN HAS A BALL

He rampaged through the Suffolk team's defence. By the 64th minute he was celebrating a hat trick. He looked full of pace and power. The ideal preparation for a trip to champions, leaders and title favourites Manchester United? Yes – except that Arsenal went on to play a different game at Old Trafford.

Sky's cameras were there again. David Hillier came in for Paul Davis. The Gunners opted for containment, with Eddie McGoldrick sweeping behind the back four. A dodgy policy, especially with a certain Eric Cantona around. The Frenchman blasted home a 25-yard free kick shortly before the break – the only goal of the game.

Arsenal pushed McGoldrick forward. Campbell and Wright went close. Graham sent on Davis and Alan Smith for the last 11 minutes. The gamble hardly had time to pay off. United held on for three points.

IT'S A STRUGGLE

Struggling Southampton arrived – minus injured ex-Gunner Perry Groves – like lambs to the slaughter. The slaughter never happened. Arsenal needed Paul Merson's overhead kick in first half injury time to earn victory against a side that hadn't won away all season.

The writing was on the wall. The Gunners were about to start a bleak goalless run.

F.A. CARLING PREMIERSHIP

RESULTS

SEPTEMBER 1

BLACKBURN ROVERS 1 (Gallacher) – ARSENAL 1 (Campbell)

SEPTEMBER 11

ARSENAL 4 (Wright, Campbell (3)) – IPSWICH TOWN 0

SEPTEMBER 19

MANCHESTER UTD 1 (Cantona) – ARSENAL 0

SEPTEMBER 25

ARSENAL 1 (Merson) – SOUTHAMPTON 0

LEAGUE POSITION

Pld	W	D	L	F	A	Pts	Pos
9	6	1	2	12	6	19	2nd

TOP LEFT:
Kevin Campbell makes it 3-0 against Ipswich with a firm header
BOTTOM LEFT:
Paul Merson's overhead kick secures three points against Southampton
BELOW:
It's hard watching from the bench . . . George Graham and Alex Ferguson at Old Trafford

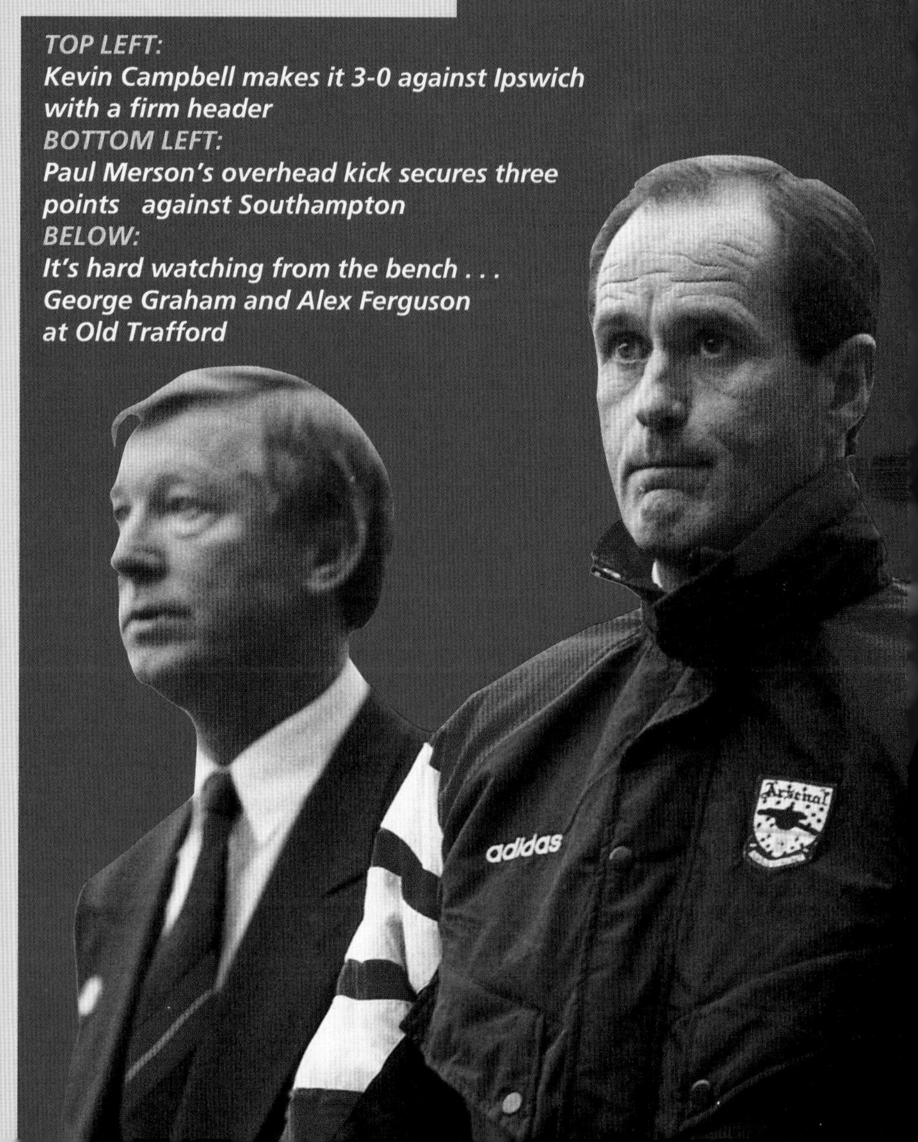

The Campbel

Kevin Campbell has added a Cup Winners' Cup medal to his set of domestic prizes. Now he aims to match Ian Wright as Arsenal's top gun in 1994/5.

That would delight both of them. They're great friends, and Ian has always been eager to sing Kevin's praises.

Campbell scored some vital goals along the road to Copenhagen – the winner against Paris St-Germain, two in the 7-0 slaughter of Standard Liège and another against Odense at Highbury.

He added 14 in the Premiership – including hat tricks against Ipswich and Swindon. Those strikes helped him to his best-ever total of 19 since he established himself during the 1990/1 title campaign.

'It was a shame Kevin didn't get 20 for the first time,' said George Graham: 'I know that was important to him. But I

is Coming!

was very pleased with him at the end of the season. He looked very lively.'

Campbell learned to play wide as Graham experimented with 4-3-3 and 4-5-1 formations. He caused PS-G all sorts of problems turning inside his markers. Now he's aiming for 20 goals-plus in 1994/5, after missing out by one on the target he set himself at the start of last season.

Bob Wilson reckons the former youth team topscorer can become one of the Premiership's most consistent marksmen. 'Kevin has been around for a while and picked up plenty of medals, so people forget he's only 24,' says the BBC commentator: 'He can still become a 30-goal-a-season striker. Andy Cole has shown what he can do for Newcastle. Kevin can do the same for Arsenal. If he becomes more confident in one-on-one situations with the goalkeeper, he'll score another ten goals a season. I have great confidence in him.'

Campbell hoped his equaliser at Sheffield United on Easter Monday would win him a place in the semi-final second leg against Paris St-Germain. It did. He responded with the winning goal, a near post header after just six minutes.

But that was a bitter-sweet night for Campbell – because Wright was booked and ruled out of the Cup Winners' Cup final.

'I didn't like to see the emotion on Ian's face after he was booked. He was so distressed,' says Kevin: 'I was very upset for him, especially because he'd helped buck me up when I needed it, after I'd taken some stick when we lost to Bolton in the F.A. Cup.'

ABOVE:
Bewigged Kevin shows off the cup, with a little help from David Hillier

LEFT:
Kevin surges powerfully in attack

OPPOSITE:
Kevin outjumps the Parma defence in Copenhagen

OCTOBER

GUNNERS FIRE BLANKS

The Arsenal forwards seemed to have left their shooting boots behind as a goal famine struck at home and away.

Four games without a goal. None conceded, none scored. If Arsenal harboured title hopes, they fled.

Lee Dixon had recovered from his ligament injury and returned at right back. The defence wasn't the problem. The Gunners might have banged home three against Standard Liege in the Cup Winners' Cup. But they couldn't score in the league.

David Seaman had hardly anything to do in the 0-0 draw at Anfield. Neither did Bruce Grobbelaar. Once that would have been an impressive result. With Liverpool in their current state of flux, it was a disappointment.

MORE POINTS DROPPED

Relegation-haunted Manchester City, in even bigger turmoil, came next at Highbury. Neil Heaney looked lively, yet City's reinforced rearguard stood firm against Arsenal's probing. It was a frustrating afternoon.

So was the trip north to frosty Oldham a week later. Seaman was a virtual spectator. The Gunners pressed forward for most of the match. But chances were few; goals non-existent. Critics blamed the lack of creativity in the Highbury midfield. It was a common complaint – though one that the Arsenal management refuted.

ABOVE:
Alan Smith attempts to break the deadlock during the goalless draw against Norwich at Highbury.

GETTING THE BIRD

George Graham was legitimately annoyed when Norwich came to Highbury. The Canaries had become the 'darlings of the media', following their UEFA Cup triumph over Germany's Bayern Munich. Having been so much on song against Bayern, they were expected to come out and play at Highbury – but they didn't. Manager Mike Walker could point to injuries but those excuses cut no ice with the Highbury crowd – particularly after the Norwich tactics in the 1-1 Coca Cola Cup draw the same week.

The Canaries' Scottish goalie Bryan Gunn was inspired. First he clawed back Alan Smith's shot just as it seemed to cross the line and then he foiled Ian Wright twice.

When Arsenal did beat the 'keeper, their efforts were off target. As more than one of the Gunners' frustrated players remarked: 'If we'd played like that away from home, we'd have been crucified on Monday morning.' But Norwich escaped with a point.

BELOW: **George Graham and Stewart Houston in lively mood during the goalless draw at Anfield**

F.A. CARLING PREMIERSHIP

RESULTS

OCTOBER 2
LIVERPOOL 0 — ARSENAL 0

OCTOBER 16
ARSENAL 0 — MANCHESTER CITY 0

OCTOBER 23
OLDHAM ATHLETIC 0 — ARSENAL 0

OCTOBER 30
ARSENAL 0 — NORWICH CITY 0

LEAGUE POSITION

Pld	W	D	L	F	A	Pts	Pos
13	6	5	2	12	6	23	3rd

NOVEMBER

BACK ON TRACK

Goals were back on the menu for Arsenal but they still had some misfortune to overcome

November opened with a mugging. That was how Aston Villa boss 'Big' Ron Atkinson truthfully described his side's 2-1 win at Highbury. 'Highway robbery' ranked among the Arsenal fans' politer descriptions.

Mark Bosnich – who saved a penalty – then substitute goalie Nigel Spink, had to withstand a constant bombardment. When Ian Wright smashed in the Gunners' first Premiership goal since September 25, the fans settled back to enjoy a rout.

Funny old game, football. Suddenly sub Guy Whittingham equalised. Then, on the stroke of time Andy Townsend netted Villa's winner.

'That's what happens when you're a tactical genius' grinned a relieved Atkinson, not believing a word!

END OF THE JINX

World Cup matches meant a fortnight's break, before Arsenal went to Chelsea. The Gunners hadn't won at Stamford Bridge since 1973/4. They broke the run this time. Andy Linighan headed down for Alan Smith to hook Arsenal ahead. Wright lashed home a penalty in first half injury time and George Graham's men were home and dry.

Drama followed at West Ham. There were 12 minutes left when the linesman didn't flag for off-side, Trevor Morley broke through – and David Seaman up-ended him outside the box.

10 MEN HOLD ON

Referee Paul Durkin reached for the red card. Off went Seaman. Graham immediately subbed Wright with reserve goalkeeper Alan Miller, who saved the resulting free kick. Somehow the Gunners held on for a goalless draw.

Steve Bould was Arsenal's hero when they beat Newcastle 2-1. The Geordies paid dearly for failing to mark him at corners. His near post header set up Wright to poke the Gunners into a 15th minute lead. Then he repeated the trick on the hour – this time with Smith applying the final touch. Peter Beardsley replied a minute later.

SINGING THE PRAISES

But Bould and Tony Adams kept a tight rein on Newcastle's top-scorer, ex-Gunner Andy Cole, and Arsenal collected three points.

The game was a fascinating clash of styles for the fans: Arsenal's power and pragmatism against Newcastle's close passing.

'The best game at Highbury this season,' said George Graham: 'And it's no coincidence that Newcastle were one of those rare teams prepared to come here and attack us.'

TOP LEFT
Alan Smith hooks home Arsenal's first goal at Chelsea

BOTTOM LEFT
Alan Smith wheels away in triumph after heading the Gunners' second goal against Newcastle

BELOW
Jubilation! Ian Wright celebrates opening the scoring against Newcastle

F.A. CARLING PREMIERSHIP
•••••RESULTS•••••

NOVEMBER 6	
ARSENAL 1 Wright	**ASTON VILLA 2** Whittingham, Townsend
NOVEMBER 20	
CHELSEA 0	**ARSENAL 2** Smith, Wright (Pen)
NOVEMBER 24	
WEST HAM UNITED 0	**ARSENAL 0**
NOVEMBER 27	
ARSENAL 2 Wright, Smith	**NEWCASTLE UNITED 1** Beardsley

•••LEAGUE POSITION•••

Pld	W	D	L	F	A	Pts	Pos
17	8	6	3	17	9	30	3rd

Highbury Ent

1993 was the year when Arsenal completed a huge part of the Highbury of the 21st century – nine months ahead of the Taylor Report deadline of August 1994.

The opening of the Clock End stand, against Newcastle on November 27, marked the end of a building programme that had been finished in little more than 18 months. And the Gunners are committed to more improvements, promises vice-chairman David Dein.

The state-of-the-art North Bank stand, holding more than 12,000 fans, opened on August 14. The Clock End followed in November, with 6,000 seats beneath the private boxes.

The Duke of Kent performed the official opening ceremony on February 15, unveiling plaques in the North Bank and at the Clock End.

Now our stadium has a capacity around 39,000, all seated. The development cost £22.5 million. The North Bank stand cost £16 million alone. But the Arsenal directors believe it's been money well spent.

Says the vice-chairman: 'The board and our design team are extremely proud of the North Bank stand. It cost a

...ers the C 21st

lot of money because we didn't want to build 'just another stand.' It's a unique development and we believe it's far better than any other stand in the country in terms of quality and facilities. We believe the North Bank stand represents the way forward for football. We tried to be innovative by adding other attractions, such as the Arsenal Museum, closed circuit TV in all public areas, well-appointed toilets, live bands before every match, customer care desks, and video games for our young supporters.'

CLOCK THAT

'We're proud of the facilities in the Clock End which are a huge improvement on what was there before. We've also put seats in the east and west lower tier paddocks, and introduced the video screens, showing the 'Arsenal TV programme' plus action replays and match highlights – a 'first' for any English club.'

'This close season we've been improving the facilities for our disabled supporters. Our next move will be to put the east and west stands under the microscope, and upgrade them as soon as possible.'

MAIN PICTURE: ***The new Clock End stand, first open in full against Newcastle on November 27***
TOP LEFT: ***Serving hungry and thirsty fans in the North Bank stand***
TOP RIGHT: ***One of the giant video screens, sited diagonally opposite at each end of the stadium***

Arsenal Arsenal Arsenal

Like so many Highbury traditions, it began with Herbert Chapman. Arsenal's great manager persuaded London Transport to change the name of the Gillespie Road tube station to 'Arsenal.' His success started a trend.

As you can see from our photos, the Gunners name has spread all over Highbury and Finsbury Park.

It's spread all over the globe too.

If you need confirmation, contact the team from Swaziland in southern Africa, who call themselves Arsenal and play in the famous red-and-white shirts.

Or call one of the Arsenal Supporters Club branches that have sprung up all over the world.

Says Supporters Club chairman Barry Baker: 'We have branches everywhere – all over Britain, in the Midlands, the North and Wales; in the Channel Islands, in Scandinavia – and much further afield.'

There's a thriving multi-racial supporters' club in South Africa, where fans of all colours idolize Ian Wright.

Australian fans have started their own club Down Under. The Scandinavian supporters – led by the redoubtable Jorn

Brekke – produce an excellent quarterly magazine, and turn up at Highbury in numbers for big games.

P.J. Gannon and colleagues ensure the Gunners maintain a high profile in Dublin. There's a west of Ireland fan club, based in Sligo.

There's no more popular English team in Malta or Cyprus.

In Chapman's glory days, it was said the name of Arsenal was famous even in the furthest corners of the earth. Only Liverpool and Manchester United have come close to matching that reputation - in the age of world-wide media.

But as Arsenal fans all know – and the signs in the neighbourhood around the ground show – there's really ONLY ONE TEAM IN LONDON.

LEFT:
Gillespie Road underground changed its name to Arsenal in the 1930.s

TOP:
The Gunners pub in Blackstock Road

BELOW:
The Arsenal Fish Bar for connoisseurs of fine fish and fine football!

AFTER A SLOW START THERE'S POST-CHRISTMAS CHEER

ABOVE:
Ian Wright congratulates Kevin Campbell on his hat trick at Swindon

The Gunners take their eyes off the ball and go down at Coventry

The bogey man of August, Mick Quinn, came back to haunt the Gunners, 11 minutes from time. Hardly the best way to prepare for the north London derby on Monday night. Sky sent their cameras again. Tottenham hadn't won a league match for weeks. But they dominated the first half and deserved the lead Darren Anderton gave them after 25 minutes.

'I can't tell you what was said in our dressing room at half time,' smiled Tony Adams afterwards.

Whatever it was, the Gunners pinned Spurs back. Anders

Limpar and Ian Wright worried them ceaselessly. Limpar set up Wright's 65th minute equaliser and Tottenham left relieved with a point.

GUNNERS LEAVE IT LATE AGAIN

Sky's *Footballers Football Show* visited Highbury the following night. The satellite crew came back again on Sunday for Arsenal v Sheffield Wednesday.

The game matched the bleak, rainswept afternoon. Many of the crowd had already left when Wright followed Andy Linighan's Wembley example and buried the Owls with a last minute goal.

Arsenal played much better at Leeds – and lost. Paul Merson was out with flu. Limpar shone in the centre of midfield. Gary McAllister scored a spectacular goal for Leeds, quickly cancelled out when Kevin Campbell deflected John Jensen's header home.

'I didn't want the first half to end, we were creating so many chances,' said Graham. Then a 49th minute hamstring injury to Smith disrupted Arsenal's rhythm. Even crueller fate awaited. Leeds' winner bounced past Seaman off Adams. And Limpar picked up a groin strain.

LATE CHRISTMAS PRESENTS

Christmas was the season to be jolly. Ray Parlour and David Hillier returned at struggling Swindon. 'We weren't trying to play offside,' said their manager John Gorman. 'Yes we were,' said his players.

It didn't matter, because Campbell and Wright cut their feeble defence to pieces. Campbell, assisted by Wright and Parlour, celebrated a hat trick in 68 minutes. Wright, not to be outdone, crashed home a dipping 35 yard shot to make it 4-0.

'Jingle bells, jingle bells,
Jingle all the way.
Oh what fun it is to see,
Arsenal win away…'

Campbell and Wright shared the goals again, when Arsenal hammered Swindon's fellow strugglers, Sheffield United, 3-0. Hillier's passes made the first two – Campbell after 11 minutes, Wright after 40. Then Campbell made certain, ten minutes after the break.

Blades' manager 'Harry' Bassett summed up his side's performance in his typically.straightforward fashion 'The way we're playing, we couldn't hit a cow's behind with a banjo…'

However, in contrast, Arsenal fans were beginning to hope the Highbury express was about to take off in pursuit of Manchester United.

ABOVE:
Ian Wright strikes a spectacular fourth goal at Swindon

LEFT:
Kevin Campbell runs to the North Bank after scoring the opening goal against Sheffield United

F.A. CARLING PREMIERSHIP

RESULTS

DECEMBER 4	
COVENTRY CITY 1 Quinn	ARSENAL 0
DECEMBER 6	
ARSENAL 1 Wright	TOTTENHAM HOTSPUR 1 Anderton
DECEMBER 12	
ARSENAL 1 Wright	SHEFFIELD WEDNESDAY 0
DECEMBER 18	
LEEDS UNITED 2 McAllister, Adams (og)	ARSENAL 1 Campbell
DECEMBER 27	
SWINDON TOWN 0	ARSENAL 4 Campbell (3), Wright
DECEMBER 29	
ARSENAL 3 Campbell (2), Wright	SHEFFIELD UNITED 0

LEAGUE POSITION

Pld	W	D	L	F	A	Pts	Pos
23	11	7	5	27	13	40	4th

JANUARY

UNDEFEATED, BUT MORE FRUSTRATION

The goal flood continued at Selhurst Park. Ten thousand travelling Highbury fans swelled the gate, and watched the Gunners demolish Wimbledon 3-0.

TOP RIGHT
Ray Parlour shoots Arsenal's second goal against Wimbledon
BOTTOM RIGHT
Gunners past and present, on opposite sides at Maine Road ... David Rocastle and Paul Merson

David Hillier made it clear, in clashes with John Fashanu and Vinnie Jones, that Arsenal wouldn't be intimidated. Kevin Campbell headed Ray Parlour's cross past Hans Segers after 18 minutes. Parlour lashed home a half-cleared corner five minutes later.

Parlour set up the third as well, finally stabbed in by Wright.

So the fans were bubbling when QPR came to Highbury on Monday. It was a case of what might have been. Kevin Campbell headed Eddie McGoldrick's corner against the bar after three minutes. Jan Stejskal saved point blank from Campbell soon after. The Czech goalie pulled off a miraculous stop from McGoldrick in the dying seconds. But Arsenal's momentum had ground to a halt.

TOO MANY DRAWS

The F.A. Cup third round meant it was 12 days before Arsenal took on Manchester City at Maine Road. Niall Quinn was out because of serious ligament damage, though City included another ex-Highbury hero, David Rocastle. The Gunners came closest to breaking the deadlock. Parlour cracked home a right foot shot – but the goal was disallowed for Campbell standing offside.

Arsenal had a record to protect when the relegation-haunted Oldham Athletic came down to Highbury. The mean Gunners' defence hadn't conceded a goal in six matches.

It wasn't long before that record changed. Graeme Sharp belted home a 25-yard drive after only four minutes and suddenly Arsenal's players knew they were in a battle.

They needed a penalty on the stroke of half-time to draw level. Referee Peter Foakes ruled Mike Milligan had handled a cross from the left, and Wright stroked home the spot kick. Oldham were furious, the Gunners elated – but all Arsenal's second half pressure came to nothing against a massed defence.

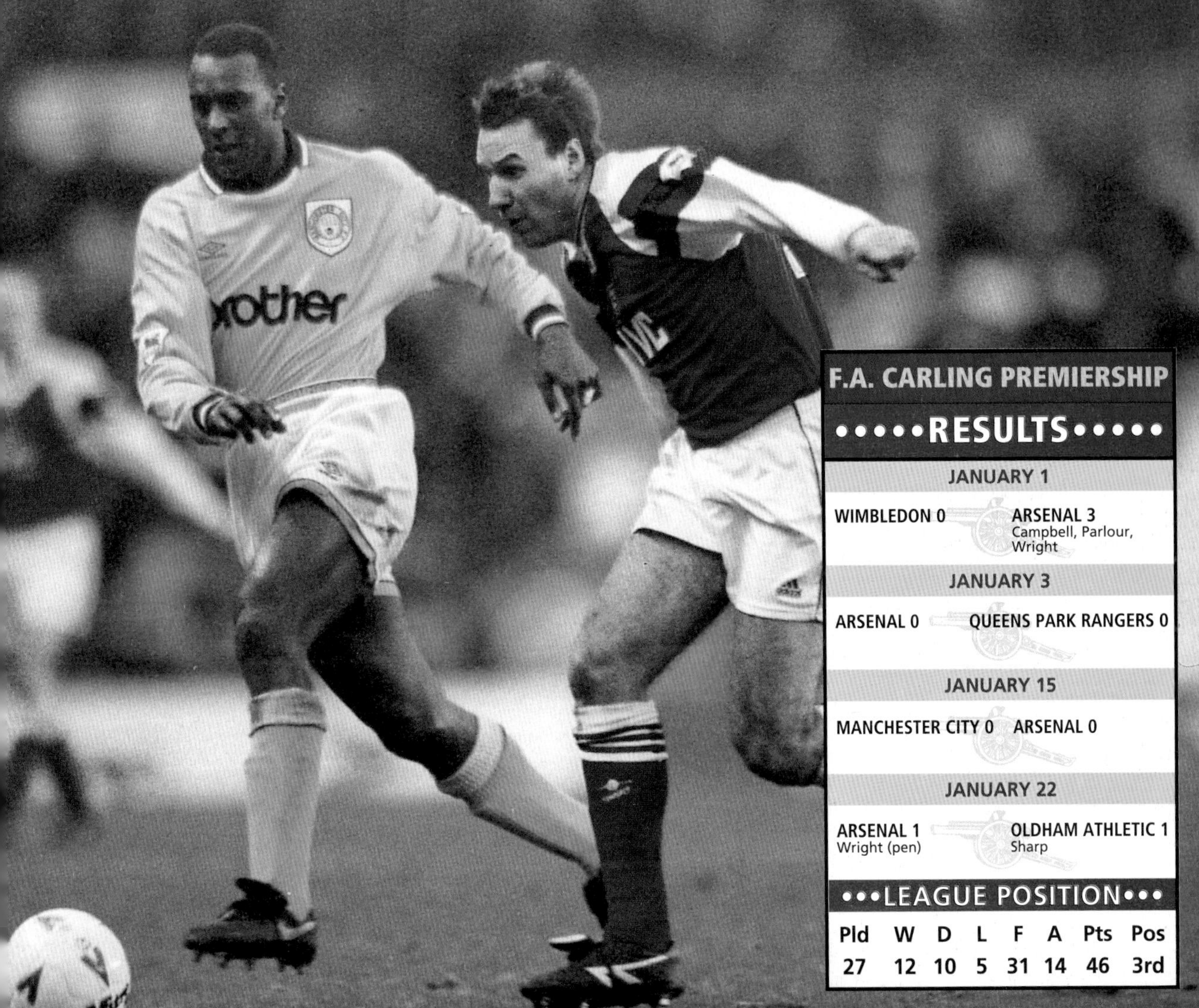

F.A. CARLING PREMIERSHIP

RESULTS

JANUARY 1

WIMBLEDON 0 — ARSENAL 3
Campbell, Parlour, Wright

JANUARY 3

ARSENAL 0 — QUEENS PARK RANGERS 0

JANUARY 15

MANCHESTER CITY 0 — ARSENAL 0

JANUARY 22

ARSENAL 1 — OLDHAM ATHLETIC 1
Wright (pen) — Sharp

LEAGUE POSITION

Pld	W	D	L	F	A	Pts	Pos
27	12	10	5	31	14	46	3rd

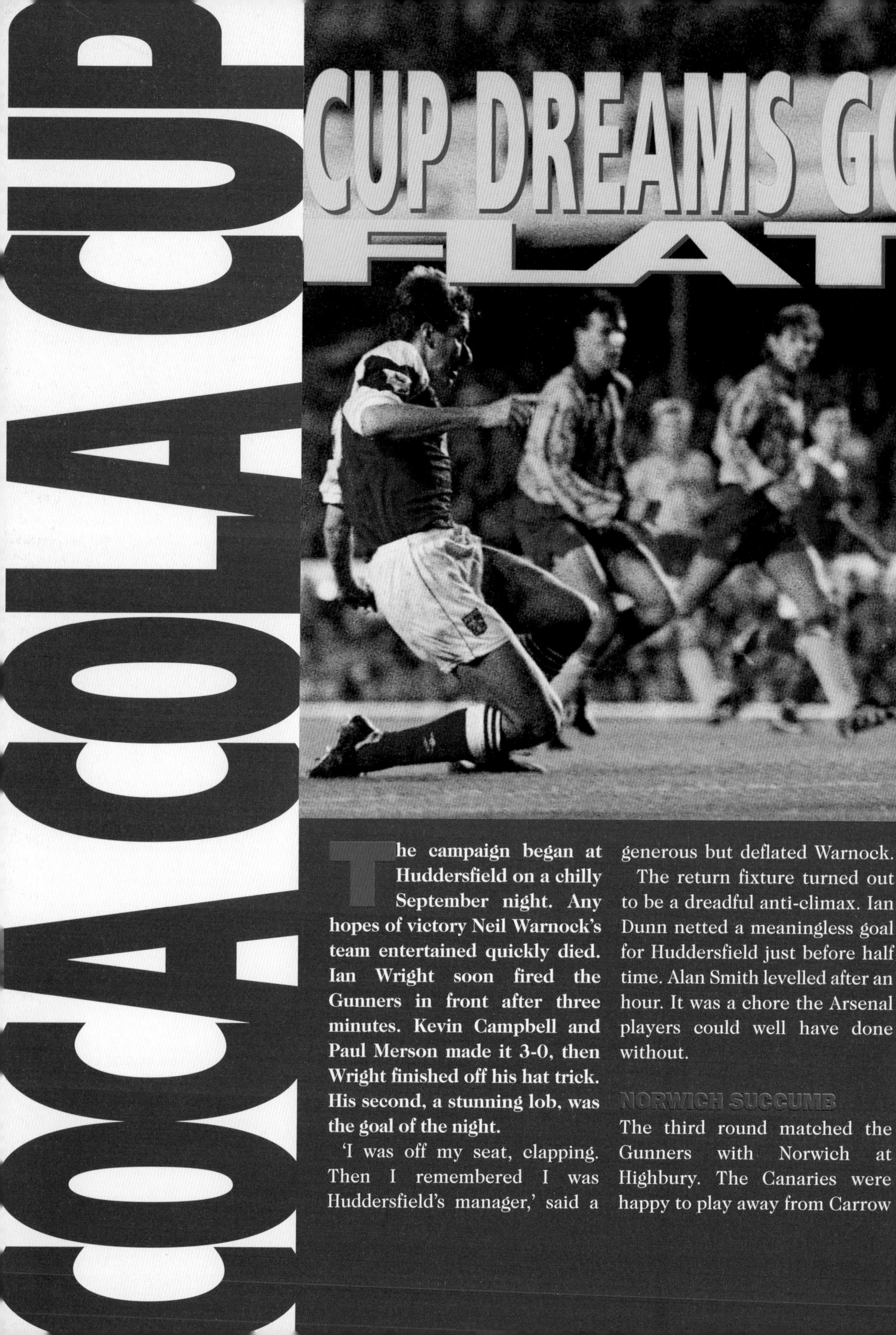

CUP DREAMS GO FLAT

The campaign began at Huddersfield on a chilly September night. Any hopes of victory Neil Warnock's team entertained quickly died. Ian Wright soon fired the Gunners in front after three minutes. Kevin Campbell and Paul Merson made it 3-0, then Wright finished off his hat trick. His second, a stunning lob, was the goal of the night.

'I was off my seat, clapping. Then I remembered I was Huddersfield's manager,' said a generous but deflated Warnock.

The return fixture turned out to be a dreadful anti-climax. Ian Dunn netted a meaningless goal for Huddersfield just before half time. Alan Smith levelled after an hour. It was a chore the Arsenal players could well have done without.

NORWICH SUCCUMB

The third round matched the Gunners with Norwich at Highbury. The Canaries were happy to play away from Carrow

The Gunners' Coca Cola defence ended in the fourth round, but there was plenty of drama along the way.

MAIN PICTURE:
Alan Smith scores against Huddersfield at Highbury

LEFT:
Ian Wright cracks the equaliser against Norwich

Road. Counter-attacking suited them perfectly. Ian Crook gave them a 33rd minute lead. Then they left Chris Sutton up front and massed in defence to protect their penalty area.

It looked mighty effective though – until Ian Wright cut in and blasted a 78th minute equaliser.

The replay was quite different. Norwich had to come out in front of their own crowd. That gave Arsenal space to get in behind them. Wright's 14th minute opener set the tone for the night.

Wright and Merson netted spectacular goals to make the final score 3-0 and booked Arsenal's place at home to Aston Villa in the fourth round.

WEMBLEY DREAMS END

Against Villa the Gunners never played. Dalian Atkinson pinched the only goal, after four minutes. Then Paul McGrath and colleagues kept Arsenal in check.

As Tony Adams said: 'We never got started.'

COCA COLA CUP
•••••RESULTS•••••

SEPTEMBER 21, SECOND ROUND (FIRST LEG)	
HUDDERSFIELD TOWN 0	ARSENAL 5 Wright (3), Merson, Campbell
OCTOBER 5, SECOND ROUND (SECOND LEG)	
ARSENAL 1 Smith	HUDDERSFIELD TOWN 1 Dunn
OCTOBER 26, THIRD ROUND	
ARSENAL 1 Wright	NORWICH CITY 1 Crook
NOVEMBER 10, THIRD ROUND REPLAY	
NORWICH CITY 0	ARSENAL 3 Wright (2), Merson
NOVEMBER 30, FOURTH ROUND	
ARSENAL 0	ASTON VILLA 1 Atkinson

FA CUP

NO DOMESTIC HONOURS THIS YEAR

It wasn't easy from the start. Arsenal had to visit George Graham's old club, Millwall in the third round – on Monday night, for Sky again. The New Den may be one of the most modern grounds in the country. But the atmosphere is just as tense as it was in the old Cold Blow Lane stadium.

George Graham used Martin Keown to tight mark the Lions' danger man Etienne Verveer. Arsenal's midfield created little. Neither did Millwall. Said David Hillier: 'They had a lot of the ball, but it didn't worry us, as long as they were playing in front of our back four.'

Tony Adams won the game, just when everyone's thoughts were turning to a replay. He headed home a corner as Merson challenged Kasey Keller. Millwall felt they'd been robbed. But Arsenal were in the fourth round.

A TOUGH ASSIGNMENT

Never under-estimate Bolton. They knocked out Liverpool in 1993 and came from 0-2 down to beat Everton in the 1994 third round replay.

Graham used Keown as a man-marker again, this time on Jason McAteer. McAteer proved a handful. So did Tony Kelly, who'd troubled the Gunners when they won at Shrewsbury in the 1991 fifth round.

McAteer escaped from Keown – who'd collided with Steve Bould – to fire Wanderers ahead. That brought Arsenal to life. Merson hit a post. Early in the second half, Wright levelled from

lerson's deflected shot, and Adams headed a second from a ree kick. It looked like Arsenal vould go through.

Bolton, however, had no inten- ion of lying down and playing lead. Bruce Rioch sent on sub Andy Walker, the fans' favourite, ınd Wanderers stepped up ınother gear. Under continual pressure the Gunners finally racked, when Owen Coyle net- ed Bolton's equaliser, only five ninutes from the final whistle.

EXTRA TIME MISERY

The replay at Highbury took a ıasty turn after 20 minutes. Phil Brown lofted an overhead kick nto the Arsenal box. The Gunners defence pressed out – ınd John McGinlay ran on to ıead past David Seaman's out- tretched hand.

Alan Smith levelled the scores, ıfter Ian Wright had challenged Aidan Davison for Lee Dixon's hrow-in. But the anxiety level ıround the stadium grew with ach passing minute, especially fter Kevin Campbell had missed two close range chances.

Disaster struck in extra time. Nigel Winterburn stubbed a back pass. Coyle's shot hit the post and McAteer buried the rebound. 5,000 Bolton fans went potty. The Arsenal supporters, resigned to their fate, left in droves. Those who remained, booed.

Walker hit a third. Kelly curled a free kick past Seaman – only to see referee Gerald Ashby disal- low it – and send off Martin Keown for a 'second bookable offence.'

It was a not a good night to be wearing red-and-white.

F.A. CUP

•••••RESULTS•••••

JANUARY 10, THIRD ROUND	
MILLWALL 0	ARSENAL 1 Adams
JANUARY 31, FOURTH ROUND	
BOLTON WANDERERS 2 McAteer, Coyle	ARSENAL 2 Wright, Adams
FEBRUARY 9, FOURTH ROUND REPLAY	
ARSENAL 1 Smith	BOLTON WANDERERS 3 McGinlay, McAteer, Walker

Don't mention Bolton at Highbury. Their name echoes like Wrexham's two years ago. Bruce Rioch's side ended Arsenal's hopes of retaining the trophy, in an extra time period that left Gunners fans cold.

ABOVE LEFT; Paul Merson and Tony Adams celebrate Tony's last minute winner at Millwall

TOP: Tony Adams heads the Gunners in front at Bolton

FEBRUARY

CHANCES ARE SQUANDERED

No game on February 5. Then came the F.A. Cup disaster at home to Bolton. So lots of eyes – as well as Sky's cameras – were trained on the Gunners when they travelled to Norwich on February 13.

Ian Wright's hamstring injury kept him out. George Graham restored John Jensen in midfield - and Paul Davis started his first game in more than three months.

Arsenal had won 3-0 at Carrow Road in the Coca Cola Cup. Hopes of a repeat rose as Graham's 4-5-1 formation dominated the first half.

Davis slipped a 33rd minute corner to Lee Dixon, who crossed beyond the far post. Alan Smith rose, nodded the ball past Bryan Gunn and Kevin Campbell netted one of the simplest tap-ins he'll ever score.

Nigel Winterburn came within inches of making it two. But half time suited Norwich more than Arsenal. Efan Ekoku blasted a 57th minute equalizer after Chris Sutton headed on Gunn's long kick. Norwich, the 'passing' team, were taking a leaf from the Highbury book.

'They make good use of the long ball . . .' said Graham, with a nod and a wink.

The Gunners ran the game again, at Everton the following Saturday. But Neville Southall was immaculate and Arsenal's finishing inaccurate. It needed a 56th minute Paul Merson spectacular – a stunning 25 yard chip – to put the Gunners ahead.

Then Mike Walker sent on Tony Cottee. Everton were roused, and Cottee pinched an equalizer nine minutes from time.

'The good thing is that we're making the chances," said Alan Smith: 'Sooner or later, we'll tuck them away and some teams will suffer.'

FLOWERS POWERS

It might have happened against Blackburn. There was a good reason why it didn't: Tim Flowers. The Rovers goalie pulled off brilliant saves from Smith, Merson and Ray Parlour as Arsenal camped around Blackburn's box in the second half.

One goal was enough, after 73 minutes. Smith crossed from the left and Merson volleyed home.

Tony Adams and Steve Bould bottled up Alan Shearer. David Seaman had so little to do he could have spent the afternoon in a deck chair.

F.A. CARLING PREMIERSHIP

RESULTS

FEBRUARY 13

NORWICH CITY 1 Ekoku	ARSENAL 1 Campbell

FEBRUARY 19

EVERTON 1 Cottee	ARSENAL 1 Merson

FEBRUARY 26

ARSENAL 1 Merson	BLACKBURN ROVERS 0

LEAGUE POSITION

Pld	W	D	L	F	A	Pts	Pos
30	13	12	5	34	16	51	3rd

BOVE:
im Flowers tips over
aul Merson's stinging shot

MAIN PICTURE:
Lee Dixon and Paul Merson celebrate Paul's winner against Blackburn

Football at Highbury is BIG

Business

For big clubs like Arsenal, gate receipts make up little more than 50% of revenue these days. The rest comes from TV money and commercial activities – and the Gunners are one of Britain's leaders in the commercial field.

Says commercial manager John Hazell: 'Arsenal have only had a commercial department since 1989 and our growth has been fantastic. Five years ago, we were looking at takings of £400,000 for merchandise. In the year ahead, we expect we'll reach around £4 million. Our first priority was to sell the Clock End boxes – then to build up our merchandising and mail order operations. Now we're challenging Manchester United and Glasgow Rangers as the British club that generates most money from commercial activities.'

'Arsenal 'World of Sport' has been our flagship, contributing about half the revenue. The Gunners Shop has been booming too – and we'll have a new, improved Gunners Shop ready for the start of 1994/5. The North Bank shop, introduced last season, has been a great success. So has our mail order department, which has grown in leaps and bounds. Our catalogues and mail shots bring in a huge number of replies. We lead the way in that field.'

Replica kit sales constitute the largest slice of Arsenal's commercial market – 35-40%. Hazell quotes figures to refute claims that children make up most of that market. 'It's not true,' he says: 'The sales ratio is three adult kits to every one bought for a child.'

John also oversees licensing agreements which control use of the club's registered trademarks. 'We want to ensure that everything sold under Arsenal's name is in keeping with the standards and traditions expected of the club,' he says.

Hazell is quick to acknowledge the debt the commercial department owes to George Graham and the team. 'Success on the field breeds revenue off it – and we've been very fortunate that George and the lads have been the most successful side in England over the last few years,' he declares.

While Hazell is looking after Arsenal's commercial activities, marketing manager Phil Carling runs the boxes, match day hospitality, the giant video screens, and the Gunners video releases.

Both agree: 'We're here to maximise revenue for the club. But it's not profit for profit's sake. The money we generate goes towards improving the team, and improving the facilities for our supporters.'

ABOVE:
Commercial Manager John Hazell

BELOW:
Marketing Manager Phil Carling

OPPOSITE:
The Gunners Shop

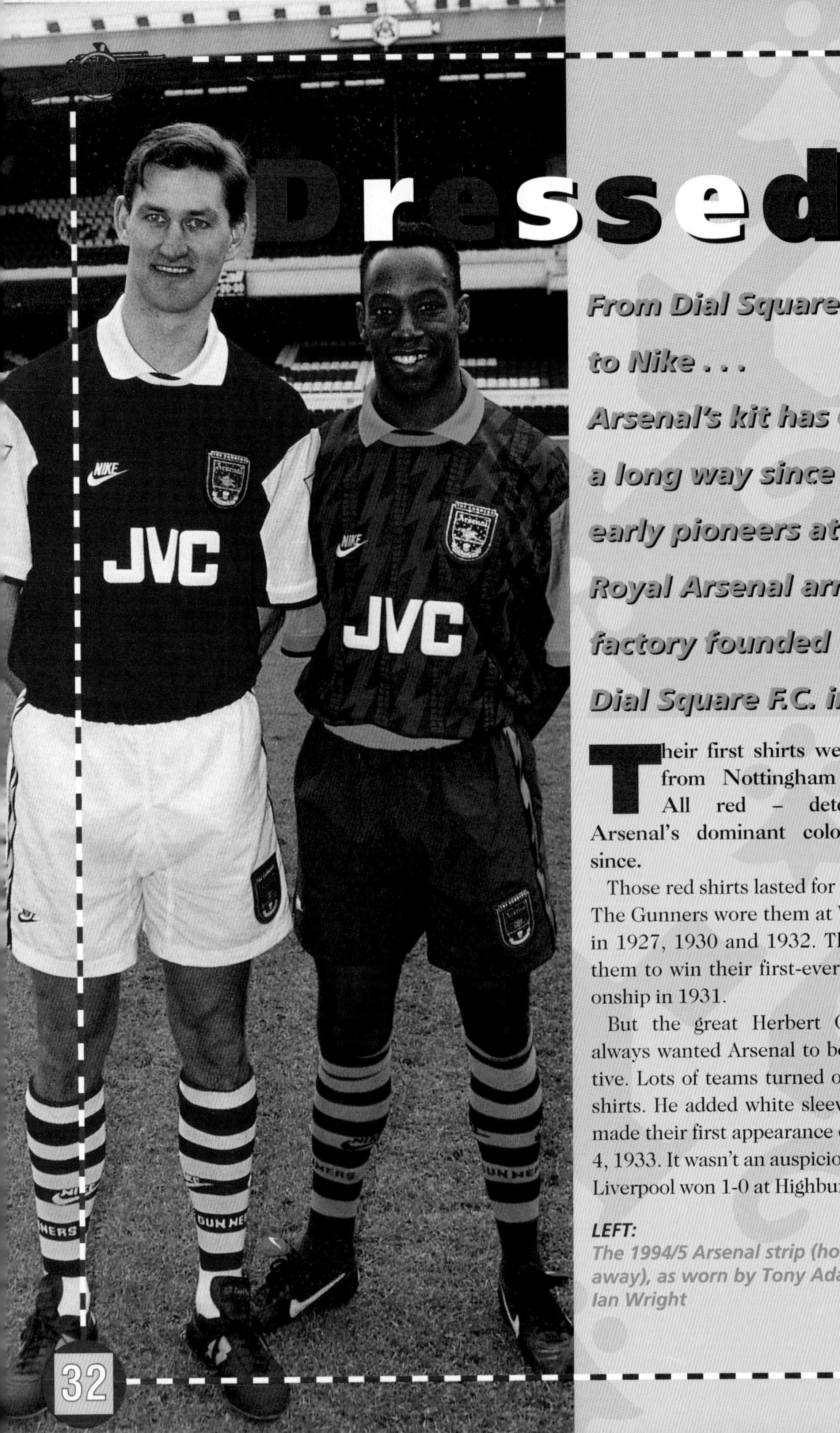

Dressed f

From Dial Square to Nike . . . Arsenal's kit has come a long way since those early pioneers at the Royal Arsenal armaments factory founded Dial Square F.C. in 1886.

Their first shirts were a gift from Nottingham Forest. All red – determining Arsenal's dominant colour ever since.

Those red shirts lasted for 47 years. The Gunners wore them at Wembley in 1927, 1930 and 1932. They wore them to win their first-ever championship in 1931.

But the great Herbert Chapman always wanted Arsenal to be distinctive. Lots of teams turned out in red shirts. He added white sleeves. They made their first appearance on March 4, 1933. It wasn't an auspicious debut. Liverpool won 1-0 at Highbury.

LEFT:
The 1994/5 Arsenal strip (home and away), as worn by Tony Adams and Ian Wright

r Success

Never mind. At the end of the season, Chapman's Gunners had clinched their second championship – the first of three-in-a-row.

The white sleeves would be linked with triumph after triumph.

That tradition moves fans even to this day. In 1965/6, Billy Wright changed Arsenal's shirts to all red again, so the Gunners wouldn't be hidebound by Chapman's legacy.

It was a forlorn move. The Gunners had to fight off relegation. Wright was sacked at the end of the season. Arsenal soon reverted to the red-and-white Highbury fans had come to expect.

There was a re-run before the Nike deal was consummated on February 17. Rumours spread that the club was about to abandon Chapman's white sleeves. Local papers publicised the protests. National media took up the story.

It certainly generated huge coverage for the kit launch.

Hey presto . . . white sleeves on the shirts as ever.

'I don't know where the stories came from,' said Arsenal's marketing manager Phil Carling, 'but they worked to our advantage. I've never seen such interest in a new strip.'

And traditionalists could sleep happy. Arsenal had kept faith with Chapman's vision.

RIGHT: *The shirt worn by Charlie George when he scored that memorable goal in the 1971 Cup Final*

LEFT: *The 1932/33 Arsenal side wearing their all-red shirts*

Matching Up To the Past

No Arsenal manager has been a keener student of the Gunners' illustrious history than George Graham.

There's a display in his office showing all the managers who've brought the championship to Highbury – from Herbert Chapman, George Allison, Tom Whitaker and Bertie Mee – to George himself.

Graham ranks among the greatest - a mighty feat, considering the competition.

Few can compare with Chapman, the man who turned Arsenal from struggling nonentities into a club famous throughout the world?

He guided Arsenal to their first major trophy, the F.A. Cup in 1930. The next season, the Gunners won the championship with a record points total; followed by a near 'double' in 1932.

RIGHT:
George Graham

Arsenal lifted the title again in 1933. They were on their way to another championship, when Chapman died so suddenly on January 6, 1934.

Allison, a director and BBC radio commentator, took over at the top, with Joe Shaw and Whittaker directing from the dressing room.

Arsenal went on to win the title in 1935 and 1938, plus their second F.A. Cup in 1936. During the war, Allison virtually ran the club on his own for seven years. He and Whittaker shared the managerial duties in 1946/7, before Allison retired.

Whittaker's first season in full charge – 1947/8 – went like a dream. The Gunners were unbeaten in their opening 17 games. They led the table from start to finish, to clinch their sixth championship. Joe Mercer was an inspired skipper and Ronnie Rooke banged home 33 goals in 42 matches.

Whittaker was offered the chance to rebuild Italian champions Torino after the Superga air crash wiped out their great team of the 40s. He turned it down to stay at Highbury. He led Arsenal to the F.A. Cup in 1950 and another championship in 1953, before the team started to break up. He died in October 1956, one of the most respected Gunners of them all.

Bertie Mee was Arsenal's physiotherapist for several years before the board made him manager after Billy Wright's departure in 1966. 'They've sent for the medicine man,' one paper wrote at the time.

Mee led Arsenal back to glory. He teamed up with some excellent coaches – Dave Sexton, Don Howe, then Steve Burtenshaw. With Don as coach, Arsenal won the Fairs Cup in 1970, and the 'double' the following season.

George Graham played in those teams. He's more than matched those achievements as Arsenal's boss.

CENTRE:
The bust of Herbert Chapman which still dominates the entrance to Highbury's marble halls

LEFT:
Bertie Mee

MARCH

PASS MASTERS

March was a good month for Arsenal. Three wins, plus a draw against the champions, as George Graham switched the squad around to keep his players fresh for Europe.

After their goalless draw in Turin, the Gunners went to Ipswich. Ian Wright had sat it out against Torino. He made Ipswich suffer. Wright scored the first. Eddie Youds turned home Anders Limpar's shot for the second. Ian netted number three from the penalty spot after Limpar had been fouled. Ray Parlour headed the fourth, then Ian outfoxed the Ipswich offside trap for his hat trick.

'We played a lot of good passing football,' grinned George Graham afterwards: 'Clearly the players weren't playing to instructions!!'

Wrighty grabbed another hat trick when Arsenal won 4-0 at Southampton, three days after knocking out Torino. His first, a diving header, was the pick of the bunch. Kevin Campbell scored the fourth, to increase Alan Ball's relegation worries.

Manchester United at Highbury the following Tuesday was a battle. Who expected anything else?

United led twice, through Lee Sharpe – but Arsenal pulled back each time. An own goal from a wicked Paul Merson free kick made it 1-1. Then Merse cracked home the shot that clinched a point. In the dying minutes, referee Vic Callow sent off Eric Cantona for a second bookable

Right: Ian Wright launches himself into a spectacular diving header, to open the score at Southampton

offence, a tackle on Tony Adams. It seemed a harsh decision, considering some of United's other 'challenges' – especially Paul Ince's lunge at Ian Selley.

FAREWELL TO ANDERS

When Liverpool arrived on Saturday, Anders Limpar had just left – in a £1.6 million move to Everton, hours before the transfer deadline. Defeat against the Reds might have had the crowd calling for him. It was never an option, even if David Seaman did make three great saves in the last 20 minutes.

The Gunners' re-shuffled side dominated for 65 minutes, then saved themselves for Paris St-Germain the following Tuesday.

Merson scored the winner, and Graham commented: 'I was delighted with his form. That's what I want – players with ability and desire."

F.A. CARLING PREMIERSHIP

RESULTS

MARCH 5	
IPSWICH 1 Dixon (o.g.)	**ARSENAL 5** Wright 3 (1pen) Parlour, Youds (o.g.)
MARCH 19	
SOUTHAMPTON 0	**ARSENAL 4** Wright 3 (1pen) Campbell
MARCH 22	
ARSENAL 2 Pallister (o.g.), Merson	**MANCHESTER UTD 2** Sharpe 2
MARCH 22	
ARSENAL 1 Merson	**LIVERPOOL 0**

LEAGUE POSITION

Pld	W	D	L	F	A	Pts	Pos
34	16	13	5	46	19	61	4th

Top: *Ian Wright tucks away the penalty at Ipswich*
Left: *The Gunners converge on Ray Parlour after he headed the fourth goal at Ipswich*

Who's the Gr... of them all

Ted Drake and Ian Wright boast fantastic strike rates. Arsenal fans will debate for ages who was the greatest striker of all.

Who's the greatest Arsenal striker of them all? The great winger Cliff Bastin leads the Gunners all-time scorers with 176. He netted those in 392 appearances. But for strike rates, few can match the two great forwards who met for the first time last November - Ted Drake and Ian Wright. Wright is signed up for three more years. If he continues to score at recent rates, Bastin's record will be under threat. Says George Graham: 'Ian can go on scoring well into his thirties. He's an excellent athlete and he has this tremendous hunger for success.'

THE RECORDS*	GAMES	GOALS
Ted Drake	182	136
Ian Wright	130	90

***not including Charity Shield**

Drake reckons if anyone can beat Bastin's figures, Ian can. Ted should know. He banged in 136 goals in just 182 appearances for the Gunners between 1934 and 1939. But for World War Two, who knows how many he'd have scored?

eatest

The days when coaches started planning to close down the opposition were far off when Drake scored all seven as the Gunners won 7-1 at Aston Villa, on December 14, 1935. When he smacked another shot against the bar and it seemed to bounce down over the line, the referee said: 'Aren't you satisfied with seven, Ted?'

Ted, now 82, joined Arsenal from Southampton for £6,500 in March 1934. He lifted the Gunners to clinch their third championship, then raced to a club record of 42 goals in 41 league games the following season - including seven hat tricks! He netted the winner in the 1936 F.A. Cup final - and set standards every Arsenal centre forward has had to match. Ted is one of Wright's biggest admirers. Ian's impact was as spectacular as Ted's. In his first season at Highbury, he pipped Gary Lineker to finish First Division top-scorer. In 1992/3, he netted 30 in all competitions. He added 34 last season - plus one in the Charity Shield.

'It's never been harder to score goals, but Ian manages it at a phenomenal rate. He's a special player,' says Drake.

The compliment delights Wright. No-one has more respect for our great centre forward of the 1930s. When Ian and Ted met, Wright handed Drake a modern Arsenal shirt signed 'To Ted, the legend.'

LEFT:
Ted admires the Arsenal Museum display on Ted the Highbury hero

ABOVE:
Ian Wright and Ted Drake, two of Arsenal's greatest goalscorers

TOP:
Ian Wright...in typical pose after another goal

Tony Adams Arsenal's Ca

Tony Adams has lifted more trophies than any captain in Arsenal's history – and he's looking forward to more, in a long career at Highbury!

When Tony hoisted the Cup Winners' Cup in Copenhagen, that made his fifth trophy in six years as skipper – including two championships, the F.A. Cup and the Coca Cola Cup.

He also played for our 1987 Littlewoods Cup-winners!

'Arsenal is a great club, a successful club – so why should I ever want to play for anyone else?' says Adams: 'We can win a lot more trophies. After proving ourselves in Europe, I'd love another championship and a crack at the European Cup.'

That commitment to the Gunners has made Tony a hero with the fans. And his displays last season earned him the nationwide recognition he's long deserved.

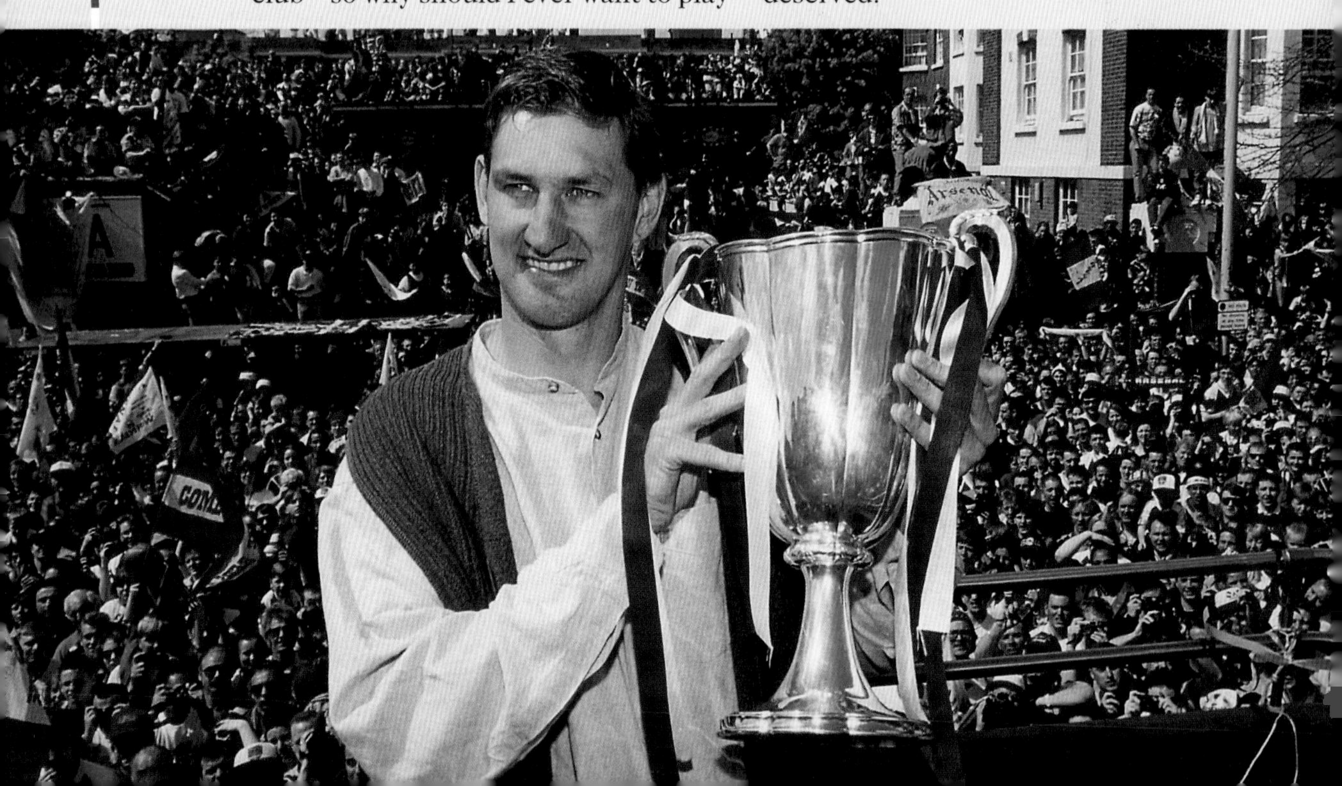

tain Marvel!

Says BBC TV commentator and 'double' team hero Bob Wilson: 'He has this terrific determination and will-to-win. He gives everything for the Arsenal. I think he's the best defender in England, and one of the best captains I've seen for a long time.'

That's no surprise to chief scout Steve Burtenshaw, who picked out Tony as a future skipper while he was still in the youth team.

Ex-assistant manager Terry Burton (now at Wimbledon) remembers Adams as a schoolboy at Highbury. 'Tony had something special about him even then,' he says: 'He was so willing to learn and so eager to get things right.'

Terry Neill gave Tony his debut – as a 17 year-old – against Sunderland in November 1983. 'I never had any doubts about him,' says the ex-Gunners boss: 'He's an inspiration to the team and the crowd.'

Capital Gold sports editor Jonathan Pearce nods in agreement. Listeners to 'London's Soccer Station' voted Adams their 'Player of the Season' for 1993/4. Says Pearce: 'I can't think of anyone who deserves it more. My co-commentator Frank McLintock was one of Arsenal's greatest captains and he's one of Tony's biggest admirers, for his qualities as a defender and a leader.'

OPPOSITE:
Tony with the Cup Winners' Cup outside Islington Town Hall

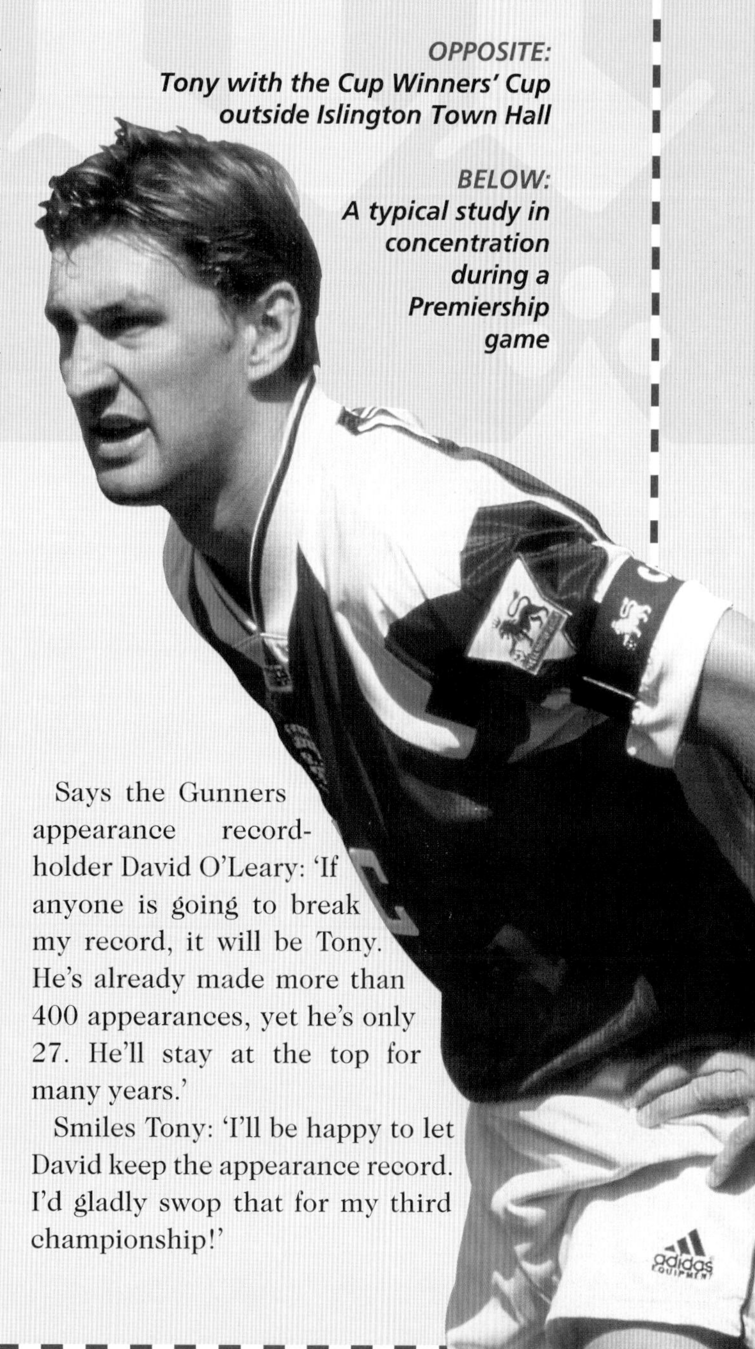

BELOW:
A typical study in concentration during a Premiership game

Says the Gunners appearance record-holder David O'Leary: 'If anyone is going to break my record, it will be Tony. He's already made more than 400 appearances, yet he's only 27. He'll stay at the top for many years.'

Smiles Tony: 'I'll be happy to let David keep the appearance record. I'd gladly swop that for my third championship!'

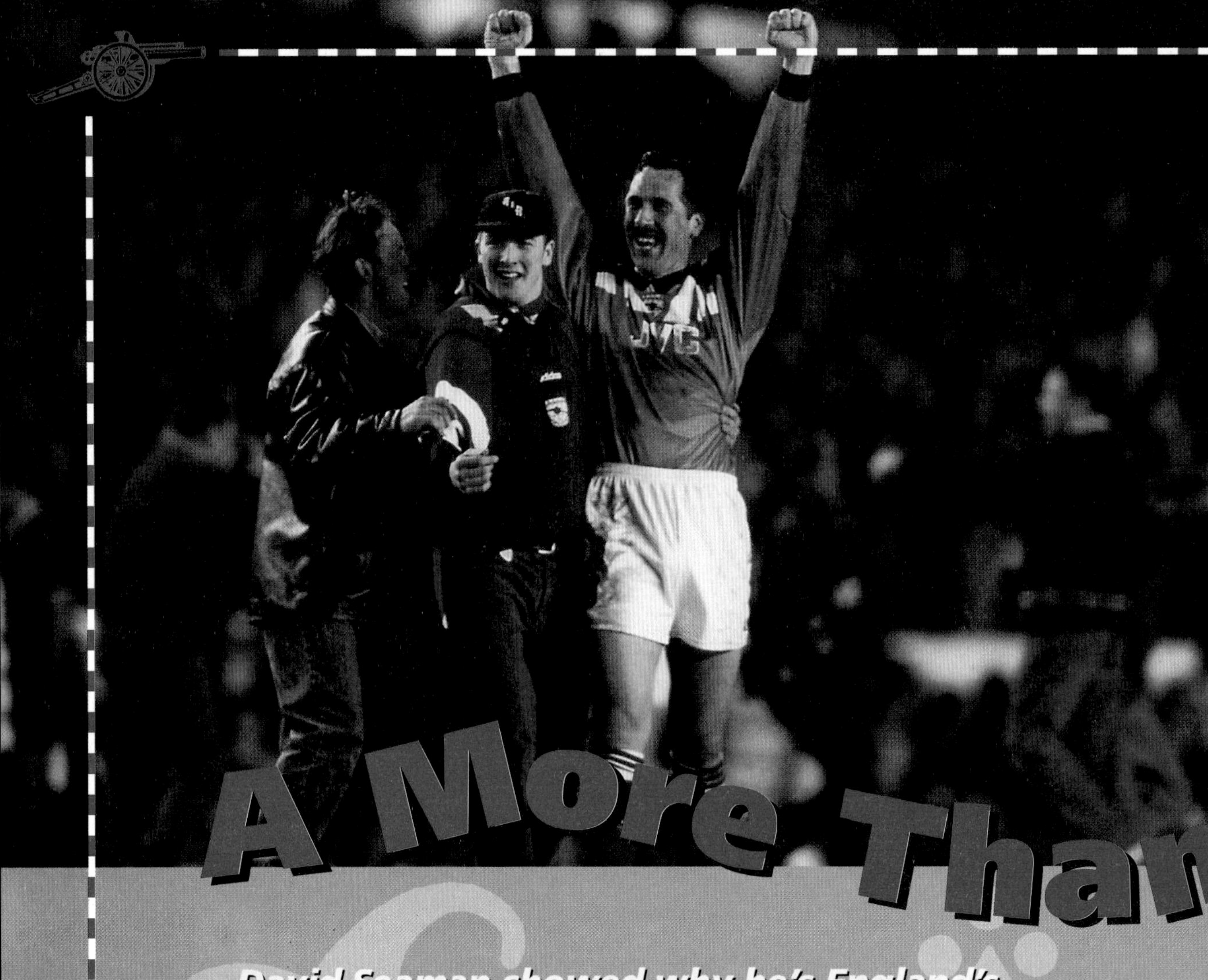

A More Than

David Seaman showed why he's England's number one goalkeeper with a brave and brilliant display in the Cup Winners' Cup final.

Seaman added a European medal to his 'set' of domestic honours. But he went through the pain barrier to do it. David was suffering from badly bruised ribs after the 1-1 draw at QPR the previous Wednesday. The pain kept him out of the match against West Ham. He needed six pain-killing injections to last 90 minutes against Parma – two before the game and four at half time.

David covered up the pain with typical calm – and pulled off a magnificent 37th minute save from Parma's top scorer, Gianfranco Zola, at the cost of jarring his ribs again.

Says Seaman: 'I watch snatches of Italian football on Sunday afternoons,

OPPOSITE TOP:
We're through! David celebrates at the end of the Cup Winners' Cup semi-final against Paris St-Germain

so I knew about Zola, Brolin and Asprilla. I'd studied videos too, in our build-up. But our defence hardly let them have a shot on target. It was a great achievement to bring home the Cup Winners' Cup. We beat some very good sides when a lot of people didn't expect us to win.'

There were ten Englishmen in the side that triumphed in Copenhagen. Several could figure in Terry Venables'

Able Seaman

new international line-up – and Seaman looks a certain starter.

Says Gunners goalkeeping coach, Bob Wilson: 'David is the top 'keeper in Britain. The best goalies are those who make the fewest mistakes, and you could count his on one hand last season.

'He's also brilliant at making saves when he's 'cold' – which is one of the hardest aspects of the goalkeeper's craft.'

Seaman's consistency has been exemplary. David's deputy, Alan Miller, has shown his potential in rare appearances. But, as Alan acknowledged, understudying the England 'keeper was one of the hardest tasks in the game.

Seaman takes a no-nonsense approach. 'It's all about concentration, and staying on guard the whole time, so I'm ready when the shots and crosses come in,' he says: 'Behind our defence, it's even more important, because I'm not in action that often! But that's what top goalkeepers get paid for. I'm not complaining. Some 'keepers say they like to be busy all the time. I'm not one. I'd much prefer us to be putting on pressure at the other end!'

ABOVE:
David carries a huge Cross of St George thrown from the Arsenal fans after the triumph in Copenhagen
OPPOSITE BOTTOM:
David launches an attack in the FA Cup Third Round game at Millwall

APRIL/MAY

CHOPPING AND CHANGING

April was a month of changes, with George Graham making four or five a match, to keep his squad fresh for the Cup Winners' Cup.

ABOVE : Ian Wright dives to head the winner against Chelsea
OPPOSITE TOP: Steve Bould cracks the leveller against Wimbledon
RIGHT: Kevin Campbell's header flies into the net for the equaliser at Sheffield United

The switching around didn't seem to bother the Gunners, at least, until April 30.

Swindon on Easter Saturday was an anti-climax after the mid-week drama in Paris. Alan Smith headed Arsenal into a fourth minute lead and the Highbury crowd settled back to enjoy a rout. It never happened. After 29 minutes, John Moncur dashed into the box and Paul Davis brought him down. Paul Bodin dispatched the penalty. Then, somehow, Swindon – with ex-Gunner Nicky Hammond in goal – survived an hour-long battering.

Kevin Campbell nodded Arsenal out of trouble at Bramall Lane on Easter Monday – a firm header from Eddie McGoldrick's near post cross to cancel out Rogers' opener for Sheffield United.

No game on April 9. Wimbledon had agreed a postponement, to help Arsenal's preparations for the semi-final second leg against Paris St-Germain.

The clash between the 'cup finalists' the following Saturday was like trench warfare. F.A. Cup finalists Chelsea came with a sweeper and a packed defence.

Sub Smith's arrival sparked the Gunners – but it needed Ian Wright's spectacular diving header to break the deadlock.

Steve Bould cracked his first goal of the season to earn a point against Wimbledon on Tuesday. Bad news was soon to come from Denmark. John Jensen had been injured against Hungary, and would miss the Cup Winners' Cup final.

VILLA'S JUST DESERTS

Wright, also to miss the final, through suspension, saw off Aston Villa – first with a crisp penalty after Neil Cox fouled him, then with a last minute winner . . . Shades of what Villa had done to Arsenal at Highbury.

Paul Merson returned after a bout of tonsilitis to crack the equaliser at QPR. But Martin Keown limped off with a hamstring injury and out of contention against Parma.

An unusual-looking Arsenal side faced West Ham in spring sunshine. The Gunners' minds were clearly on Copenhagen and no more injuries. Trevor Morley and Martin Allen took advantage in the closing minutes.

Ex-Gunner Andy Cole, the Premiership topscorer, and Peter Beardsley, scored the goals that beat tired Arsenal at Newcastle. Alan Miller made some great saves. But the scoreline hardly mattered.

The Gunners had already beaten Parma in Copenhagen.

F.A. CARLING PREMIERSHIP

•••••RESULTS•••••

Date	Home	Away
APRIL 2	ARSENAL 1 Smith	SWINDON TOWN 1 Bodin (pen)
APRIL 4	SHEFFIELD UTD 1 Rogers	ARSENAL 1 Campbell
APRIL 16	ARSENAL 1 Wright	CHELSEA 0
APRIL 19	ARSENAL 1 Bould	WIMBLEDON 1 Earle
APRIL 23	ASTON VILLA 1 Houghton	ARSENAL 2 Wright 2 (1pen)
APRIL 27	QPR 1 Penrice	ARSENAL 1 Merson
APRIL 30	ARSENAL 0	WEST HAM UNITED 2 Morley, Allen
MAY 7	NEWCASTLE UNITED 2 Cole, Beardsley (pen)	ARSENAL 0

•••LEAGUE POSITION•••

Pld	W	D	L	F	A	Pts	Pos
42	18	17	7	53	28	71	4th

Nigel Winter 'Mr Consiste

It's hard to think of a more consistent Gunner than Nigel Winterburn. That's why the Arsenal staff looked fraught when the ex-Wimbledon left back was carried off in the dying minutes of the semi-final win over Paris St-Germain.

That's why they were delighted he came through a reserve run-out against Bristol City and the Premiership match against West Ham, to prove his fitness for the Cup Winners' Cup final.

That's why they were worried when Nigel was poleaxed by a cross that hit him in the face during the closing minutes in Copenhagen – and they watched anxiously as Nigel narrowly escaped the coins flung from the Parma end while Gary Lewin was treating him

But Winterburn recovered to finish the 90 minutes and claim another medal. Two championships, the F.A. Cup, the Coca Cola Cup and the Cup Winners' Cup make an impressive tally.

'I had to test myself before the final because you can't walk straight into a game like that,' said Nigel: 'You have to be 100% right, to do justice to yourself, and the team.'

Winterburn knows he might have missed the final. His sympathy goes out

TOP LEFT:
Anxious moments for Nigel as he's treated by Gary Lewin during the final – and the Gunners have to dodge missiles from the Parma end

...burn

...cy'

to those who did – Ian Wright (suspended) and injured John Jensen, David Hillier and Martin Keown.

Says Nigel: 'Every time we reach a final, someone seems to miss out. David's been really unlucky. He's missed out two years running now. It's heart-breaking to sit out such big games. So I really appreciate my medal from Copenhagen.'

The win over Parma was one of the high points in Winterburn's 300-plus appearances for the Gunners, since his £350,000 move from Wimbledon in the summer of 1987.

In his early days at Highbury – with England's Kenny Sansom established at left back – Nigel often played on the right. It wasn't a comfortable role for a left-footed player. But he didn't have long to wait.

Winterburn took over as the Gunners number three at the start of the 1988/9 title campaign. 'I feel happy now, because I'm playing in my best position,' he said at the time. He's never looked back – though he's had to overcome spasms of back trouble along the way.

ABOVE:
1-0 to the Arsenal . . . Nigel enjoys himself after the final whistle in Copenhagen

Nigel is one of Arsenal's quiet men. His philosophy is simple. 'I just try and be as consistent as I can,' he says. It's served him well in seven years with the Gunners.

Stewart Und
PRES

First team coach Stewart Houston is a rarity among the Gunners' coaching staff. He didn't play for Arsenal!

The former Manchester United left back has become a Gunner through and through, since arriving at Highbury as reserve team coach in 1987.

He's also seen the pressure from inside, at two of the world's most famous clubs.

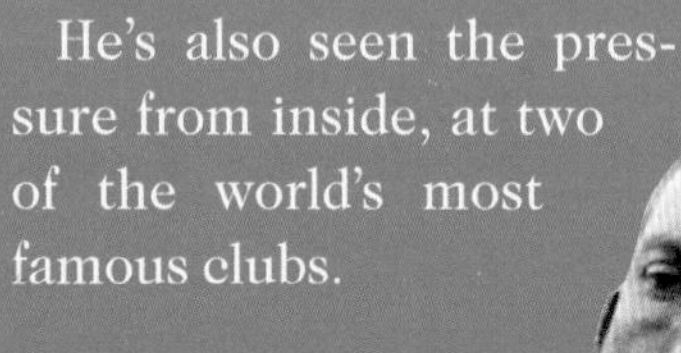

In 1990, Stewart led the reserves to the Combination title, then stepped up to become first team coach. Since then, Arsenal have won the championship, F.A. Cup, Coca Cola Cup and the Cup Winners' Cup.

Houston played a big part in the Cup Winners' Cup triumph. Not just onthe

rstands the
URES

training ground, but also with his shrewd assessment of opponents – a job he shared with 'spying' colleagues Steve Burtenshaw and Steve Rowley.

'Manchester United have always been popular with the media. That's not been the case with Arsenal. So I was pleased to see the players getting the credit they deserved, at the end of our European run,' says Stewart.

'I'd had a long look at Parma and I knew how good they were. So it was a great performance in Copenhagen. All our players were heroes that night.'

It 's ironic that the only other English club to win a Euro trophy since the Heysel ban was revoked are Manchester United, who lifted the Cup Winners' Cup in 1991.

'What is expected of clubs like Arsenal and Manchester United is success. Current sides are continually compared with the great teams of the past. It was a burden at Old Trafford for years, because – until 1993 – the players were continually reminded that United hadn't won the title since 1967,' says Stewart.

'It's the same at Highbury. Arsenal have been the most consistent team in England over the last five or six seasons, yet fans inevitably compare the present squad with the sides that won the championship in 1989 and 1991.'

'Supporters of every other club in England would love to have won what Arsenal have won! They're the standards we have to live up to. After Copenhagen, though, I'm sure our fans are looking forward to 1994/5!'

OPPOSITE TOP:
Bringing home the cup . . . Stewart Houston (left) with George Graham and physio Gary Lewin

OPPOSITE BOTTOM:
Stewart puts his back into it in training

ABOVE:
Stewart oversees squad training in Copenhagen

Steve Bould Rock of the

Terry Venables recognised Steve Bould when he named him for his England debut against Greece on May 17.

It was the England boss's reward for the 31 year-old defender's contribution to the Gunners' successes, since his £390,000 move from Stoke in the summer of 1988.

Despite two long spells out because of groin trouble – one which cost him appearances in the 1993 Wembley finals – Steve has helped Arsenal win two titles, and the Cup Winners' Cup.

The man George Graham calls 'our colossus' had to fight back from injury again – a thigh problem this time – to regain his place alongside Tony Adams last November.

Steve's return meant Arsenal lined up with the same back four that conceded just 18 goals on the way to the 1991 championship. The Gunners finished the Premiership's tightest defence, letting in just 28 goals.

Adams paid tribute to Steve after the Cup Winners' Cup quarter-final win over Torino. Said Tony: 'Steve was excellent. David Seaman didn't have one shot to save. That says it all. And Steve's been playing like that ever since he came back.'

Bould's display in Copenhagen was almost faultless. He set the tone in the opening seconds, when Faustino Asprilla broke through – and Steve dived in to halt him.

Says Bould: 'I had an operation at the start of last season, so I

Defence

couldn't have asked for anything better than the way things worked out.'

'I felt for the players who missed the final against Parma. My groin problems kept me out of the Coca Cola and F.A. Cup finals against Sheffield Wednesday. So I know how they felt. Football can be a cruel game.'

The Gunners triumph in Copenhagen lifted hopes for 1994/5. So did a run of 19 league games unbeaten. Steve is optimistic Arsenal can sustain another title assault.

'Manchester United are a very good team and they got it right last season. They have a strong defence plus a lot of flair players in midfield and up front. But we played really well in the second half of the season. If we'd been in that form earlier, we'd have pushed them much harder,' he says: 'I hope we carry on where we left off!'

Steve Bould – always alert in defence

Just another day at the office as Steve dominates the Spurs attack

Steve Bould (back, third from left) . . . a key figure in Arsenal's successes since 1988

The Road to

From Odense to Paris St-Germain . . . how the Gunn

It all began on a filthy wet night in Odense. Tony Adams was suspended – and Arsenal's Cup Winners' Cup hopes nearly died before they'd started. The Danes scored first then they missed a penalty, and for 20 minutes the Gunners were all over the place.

Arsenal pulled themselves together. Ian Wright equalised. Paul Merson broke away to hit the winner. 'That was with my left foot – shouldn't it count double?' joked Merse afterwards. But the Gunners knew they'd escaped from the brink of disaster.

The second leg was a non-event. Kim Brink's team made life difficult. They even equalised Kevin Campbell's header. But Arsenal eased through to the second round.

Enter Standard Liège from Belgium. Ian Wright tore them apart at Highbury. Merson scored a brilliant free kick. The Standard manager, Arie Haan, was sacked a few days later. So was his replacement, Rene van der Eycken, after Arsenal slaughtered Standard 7-0 in Liège. Alan Smith, Merson, Tony Adams, Kevin Campbell(2), Ian Selley and Eddie McGoldrick helped themselves, while Ian

Copenhagen

eached their first European final for 14 years

Wright watched from the sidelines.

Torino in the quarter-final posed some tougher questions. George Graham won the tactical battle in Turin, stationing David Hillier in front of Adams and Steve Bould to stop Enzo Francescoli and sub Benito Carbone breaking from midfield. Arsenal created most of the chances. Many thought a goalless draw did the Gunners less then justice.

The Torino coach Emiliano Mondonico reckoned his team could win at Highbury. They didn't try, until they fell a goal behind. Paul Davis's perfectly flighted 66th minute free kick found Adams at the far post, and Tony headed the only goal of the game.

French league leaders Paris St-Germain thought they were technically superior to Arsenal. So they were shocked when the Gunners took command at the Parc des Princes. Their goalkeeper Bernard Lama was PS-G's hero. Wright beat him once to head Arsenal in front. Lama made miraculous saves from John Jensen and Alan Smith. And PS-G punished rare slackness on the Gunners' near post at a corner, when David Ginola sneaked in to head the equaliser.

PS-G pulled out the stops at Highbury. Valdo, the Brazilian, buzzed in midfield. Adams was remarkable; organising, calming, dashing in with last ditch tackles. The French threatened, but Seaman was rarely troubled.

Campbell's sixth minute header from Lee Dixon's cross proved decisive.

OPPOSITE LEFT: *Ian Wright slips the ball past Standard Liège goalkeeper Jacky Munaron, to make it 3-0 at Highbury*
CENTRE: *Kevin Campbell heads the only goal against Paris St-Germain at Highbury*
TOP: *Tony Adams heads the winner against Torino*
BELOW: *Paul Merson, Eddie McGoldrick and Kevin Campbell celebrate after the Gunners 7-0 romp in Liège*

CUP WINNERS' CUP

Wonderful, Wonderful Copenhagen

'One-nil to the Arsenal! One-nil to the Arsenal!' The words rang around Copenhagen's Parken Stadium as the Gunners celebrated their first European trophy since 1970.

Typically, Arsenal won it the hard way: with Ian Wright suspended; John Jensen, Martin Keown and David Hillier injured.

They all pitched into the party at the final whistle – even the limping JJ, who left his Danish TV position to celebrate with his jubilant colleagues.

There were times when the Gunners rode their luck. Steve Bould had to launch a last ditch tackle on Faustino Asprilla in the opening seconds. Tomas Brolin hit the inside of a post. David Seaman made a blinding save from Gianfranco Zola.

Those incidents have been long forgotten. But one moment will stick in the memory forever: Alan Smith, pouncing on Lorenzo Minotti's misdirected clearance then cracking a left footed 20 yarder past Luca Bucci, off a post.

It was a great night for George Graham, enjoying European success as a manager to add to his Fairs Cup winners' medal 24 years ago.

It was a great night for 12,000 Arsenal fans in the stadium and thousands more around the world.

And it was a great night for 'Smudge'.

He was George Graham's first major signing – an £850,000 snip from Leicester. Smith has netted two championships; F.A. Cup and Coca Cola winners medals; more than 100 goals, and two 'Golden Shoe' awards.

But he's never played better than he did in Copenhagen.

'I was delighted for Alan. It wasn't just that he scored the goal. He was the outstanding play-

er on the night and an inspiration to everyone. He worked tirelessly to hold the ball up,' said Graham.

It was a special night for other Gunners too – for young Ian Selley, for the veteran Paul Davis, whose experience proved so valuable in Europe, and for Coca Cola Cup final hero Stephen Morrow, called up at the last minute to chase and harry Parma's stars.

Parma coach Nevio Scala was generous to the Gunners. 'Arsenal played a very clever and organised game,' he said: 'Our players were never allowed to settle.'

'Smudge'? 'It was a fantastic way to end the season,' he grinned: 'To beat a side of Parma's calibre was a great boost to us all. And to score the winner ranks among the top achievements of my career!'

OPPOSITE:
Smudge lifts the cup!
TOP:
The happy Gunners at the end!
ABOVE:
Alan Smith cracks home the winning goal
ABOVE:
Steve Morrow takes the ball away from Parma star Tomas Brolin

THE ROAD TO SUCCESS

•••••RESULTS•••••

SEPTEMBER 15, 1st round 1st leg	
ODENSE 1 Keown (o.g.)	**ARSENAL 2** Wright, Merson
SEPTEMBER 29, 1st round 2nd leg	
ARSENAL 1 Campbell	**ODENSE 1** Nielsen
OCTOBER 20, 2nd round 1st leg	
ARSENAL 3 Wright (2), Merson	**STANDARD LIÈGE 0**
NOVEMBER 3, 2nd round 2nd leg	
STANDARD LIÈGE 0	**ARSENAL 7** Smith, Campbell(2), Adams, Selley, Merson, McGoldrick
MARCH 2, Quarter Final 1st leg	
TORINO 0	**ARSENAL 0**
MARCH 15, Quarter Final 2nd leg	
ARSENAL 1 Adams	**TORINO 0**
MARCH 29, Semi-Final 1st leg	
PARIS ST-GERMAIN 1 Ginola	**ARSENAL 1** Wright
APRIL 12, Semi-Final 2nd leg	
ARSENAL 1 Campbell	**PARIS ST-GERMAIN 0**
MAY 4, Final at Parken Stadium, Copenhagen	
ARSENAL 1 Smith	**PARMA 0**

JJ Helps Arsenal Bring Home the Bacon!

One of the great memories of that night when fairy tales came true in Copenhagen was of John Jensen, dancing across his home soil despite a limp, as happy as if he'd scored the winning goal.

It was consolation for Jensen, one of the Gunners' ever-presents in Europe, crocked a fortnight before the main event.

JJ, who joined Arsenal from Danish club Brondby, had been so looking forward to playing in the final, in the city where he was born.

That was before Jensen's season was cut short by a lunge from Hungary's Gabor Halmai in the same Parken Stadium on April 20. 'George Graham did me a favour by letting me go to play

ABOVE:
JJ talks to Danish TV before the final

ABOVE LEFT:
JJ congratulates Arsenal's hero Alan Smith

It looks like a goal all the way for John Jensen in Paris

INSET:
But somehow, PS-G goal-keeper Bernard Lama makes a brilliant save

for Denmark, then it all turned sour,' recalls JJ: 'I knew it was bad. I knew at once, the final was gone. I can't understand why the Hungarian didn't get a red card.'

'But at least I was able to be out on the pitch at the end of the final, holding up the trophy and shouting 'We won the Cup' along with the rest of the lads!'

Now the 29 year-old Dane's sights are set on more prizes in 1994/5, to add to his 1993 F.A. Cup winner's medal – and, maybe, his first goal for the Gunners.

JJ has become a Highbury folk hero in the Willie Young tradition, even though – or perhaps, because – he's yet to score in 81 appearances.

'Everyone has talked about it. The players, the press, the supporters – even my mum and dad have joked about it,' he says.

Probably the closest he's come was in the semi-final first leg in the Parc des Princes. Jensen's 25-yarder looked a winner all the way – until Paris St-Germain goalie Bernard Lama pulled off a miraculous save.

'Maybe in the new season . . .' says JJ: 'But I'm not bothered if I don't score at all, as long as we win. If I go home to Denmark with some medals at the end of my contract, I'll be very happy. I'm more of a defensive midfielder than an attacker, and I've played some good games in that role.'

'I think our fans appreciate that, They've been very good to me – and if I do score, I'm sure they'll mark the occasion!'

LEE DIXON
Upsetting t

Lee Dixon reckons the Gunners had an extra incentive to win the Cup Winners' Cup – for suspended Ian Wright and casualties, John Jensen, Martin Keown and David Hillier.

The Gunners who missed the final in Copenhagen will receive replica medals. But Dixon sympathises with them all.

Says Lee: 'You can't imagine what they're feeling, sitting on the sidelines, unless you've been through it. It happened to me when I missed the 1993 Coca Cola Cup final through suspension. But that wasn't as bad, because I still had the F.A. Cup final to come.'

'To get injured, or suspended, for the big occasion is a much bigger blow. It was even harder for JJ, because the final was in Denmark. And David Hillier has now missed out on three cup finals because of injury.'

Yet youngsters like Ian Selley and deputies like Stephen Morrow did remarkable jobs in Copenhagen.

ABOVE LEFT:
We've scored! Lee celebrates Alan Smith's goal against Parma

e Odds

That never surprised Dixon. Before the final, he predicted: 'We have players to slot in. They've never let us down and I'm sure they won't against Parma.'

Lee knows all abut upsetting the odds. Victory in Copenhagen meant a European triumph to add to two championships and an F.A. Cup winners medal. But he's had to battle all the way.

Burnley gave him a free transfer as a youngster. He moved on to Chester, then – for £3,500 – to Bury, where ex-Burnley pair Martin Dobson and Frank Casper were in charge. That was where his career took off. Stoke paid £40,000 for him, and George Graham swooped with a £350,000 bid in January 1988.

'When you've been around the lower divisions, it makes you appreciate a club like Arsenal,' says Lee: 'As a team, we've had to prove a lot of people wrong too.'

'I've got used to the criticism over the last six years. Yet it's helped us build up an inner strength. When we're written off, we bounce back, because we're determined to confound our critics. We weren't given much of a chance in Copenhagen either. The situation brought the best out of us. Sometimes I suspect we rather relish being the 'rogues' of English football!'

'Maybe that's changing though. I think the media, and fans of other clubs, appreciate what we've done for English football by bringing home the Cup Winners' Cup.'

ABOVE: *Where did you get that hat? Delighted Lee after the final whistle in Copenhagen*

BELOW: *Lee picturedwith Eddie McGoldrick after the Cup Winners' Cup triumph*

George Look[s to the] FUTU[RE]

Even as Arsenal were celebrating the Cup Winners' Cup final triumph over Parma, George Graham was turning his thoughts to 1994/5.

After guiding the Gunners to their first European trophy for 24 years, George has set his sights even higher – on the European Cup.

Before then, Graham aims to pilot Arsenal to their 11th title, and retain the Cup Winners' Cup.

'It will be harder to retain the trophy than to win it – but why not!' he says: 'The players have been magnificent. They've shown tremendous flexibility to cope with all sorts of European styles – and tremendous resilience. We can do it again.'

'But winning the championship is what matters most. I'm looking to strengthen our squad, and I want us to be right up there with Manchester United at the top.'

'Another championship would also land us another shot at the European Cup. That's the only major trophy Arsenal have never won. After what we've learned in Europe, we'd be well-equipped to go for it.'

ABOVE LEFT:
George gets his hands on another trophy!

to the RE

George, in thoughtful mood before the semi-final in Paris

After six trophies in eight years, Graham ranks with Tom Whittaker and the legendary Herbert Chapman as Arsenal's greatest manager.

Another chance to win the European Cup appeals to George's sense of history. So does that comparison with the giants of the Gunners' past.

Go to an auction of football memorabilia – and you'll probably find the 1971 'double' hero bidding for every item with an Arsenal connection. Few appreciate the Gunners traditions more.

George wanted to found a dynasty of success, like Chapman and Whittaker built between 1930 and 1953. Since he arrived, in May 1986, he's led Arsenal to two championships, two League Cups, the F.A. Cup and a European trophy. He's transformed the club. First by winning the League Cup in 1987, and turning a £1.2 million deficit into a healthy profit. Then by making Arsenal the most consistent team in England.

He's transformed the fans expectations too. Before he returned, they only dreamed of championships. Now, the Gunners are expected to win a trophy every season.

Graham and his troops usually deliver.

BELOW: George, Tony Adams and Alan Smith bring home the cup at Stansted airport

Young Guns are Blazing

'Three-nil to the Arsenal...' On May 12, the song lauded the Gunners youngsters - who came from behind to beat Millwall 5-3 on aggregate and lift the F.A. Youth Cup.

It was Arsenal's fourth Youth Cup triumph. Pat Rice's youngsters emulated their predecessors in 1966, 1971 and 1988. Rice played in the 1966 success, and coached the 1988 side.

'It was a great night and I was delighted for the boys. Now I hope they'll climb all the way up the ladder,' he grinned, as skipper Matthew Rose waved the cup to a cheering crowd of nearly 5,000.

Matthew Rawlins and Gavin McGowan had each equalised for Arsenal in the first leg at the New Den. But Mark Kennedy's goal two minutes into injury time earned Millwall a 3-2 lead to protect at Highbury.

The young Gunners grabbed the opening goal after 22 minutes. Rawlins leapt like a salmon to flick on a corner, and Tony Clarke's head planted the ball into the net.

RIGHT:
Tony Clarke... scored the first goal in the final at Highbury
ABOVE LEFT:
The young Gunners celebrate their F.A. Youth Cup final triumph over Millwall

Arsenal had to wait until the 70th minute to grab the aggregate lead. Stephen Hughes chipped a neat free kick and Rawlins met it at the far post with a perfect header.

Noel Imber made three brilliant saves as the Lions desperately tried to force extra time. Referee Rushden allowed five minutes for stoppages. Then Hughes finished the argument, with a crashing left foot volley from Michael Black's free kick.

Said Rice: "We only had five second year boys in the squad - Matthew Rose, Gavin McGowan, Graeme Hall, Chris McDonald and Matthew Rawlins. Graeme and Gavin were injured earlier in the season. So what the lads did is a terrific achievement.

'We gave some great performances along the way. The fourth round at Burnley was the turning point. The lads were magnificent under constant pressure. After that win, they started thinking: 'we can win this.'

'In the quarter-final, we beat Stoke, who were well-fancied; then Bradford twice – and they'd knocked out Manchester United and Blackburn.'

'What matters now, is how many players progres to the first team. Kevin Campbell, David Hillier, Stephen Morrow and Alan Miller all made it through from the 1988 side and Neil Heaney went to Southampton for a sizable fee. That's what youth football is about – developing first team players.'

F.A. YOUTH CUP
•••••RESULTS•••••

ROUND 2

v
COLCHESTER (a) 3-2
scorers: Rankin, Rawlins, Rose

ROUND 3

v
BRENTFORD (a) 1-1
scorer: Black

ROUND 3 replay

v
BRENTFORD (h) 3-1
scorers: Dennis, Hughes, Rawlins

ROUND 4

v
BURNLEY (a) 1-0
scorer: Rawlins

ROUND 5

v
STOKE (h) 3-1
scorers: Clarke, Rose, Howell

SEMI-FINAL first leg

v
BRADFORD (a) 1-0
scorer: McGowan

SEMI-FINAL second leg

v
BRADFORD (h) 1-0
scorer: Hughes

FINAL first leg

v
MILLWALL (a) 2-3
scorers: Rawlins, McGowan

FINAL second leg

v
MILLWALL (h) 3-0
scorers: Clarke, Rawlins, Hughes

•••TEAM AGAINST MILLWALL•••
at Highbury

Imber, Griggs, Taylor, Clarke, Hall, McDonald, Black, Rose (Howell, 71 minutes**), Rawlins (Drake,** 83 minutes**), McGowan, Hughes**

ABOVE: *Pat Rice*

LEFT: *Stephen Hughes... his goal finished off the Lions challenge*

ROLL OF HONOUR

LEAGUE CHAMPIONS

1931, 1933, 1934, 1935, 1938, 1948, 1953, 1971, 1989, 1991

RUNNERS-UP: 1926, 1932, 1973

F.A.CUP WINNERS

1930, 1936, 1950, 1971, 1979, 1993

RUNNERS-UP: 1927, 1932, 1952, 1972, 1978, 1980

LEAGUE CUP WINNERS

1987, 1993

RUNNERS-UP: 1968, 1969, 1988

UEFA CUP WINNERS

1970

EUROPEAN CUP WINNERS' CUP

1994

RUNNERS-UP: 1980